The Unbelievable Origins of Snake Oil
and Other Idioms

by Arnold Ringstad • illustrated by Dan McGeehan

Published by The Child's World®
1980 Lookout Drive • Mankato, MN 56003-1705
800-599-READ • www.childsworld.com

Acknowledgments
The Child's World®: Mary Berendes, Publishing Director
The Design Lab: Design and production
Red Line Editorial: Editorial direction

Design elements: Kirsty Pargeter/iStockphoto

ISBN 9781614732389
LCCN 2012932810

Printed in the United States of America
Mankato, MN
July 2012
PA02118

Contents

TOP NOTCH

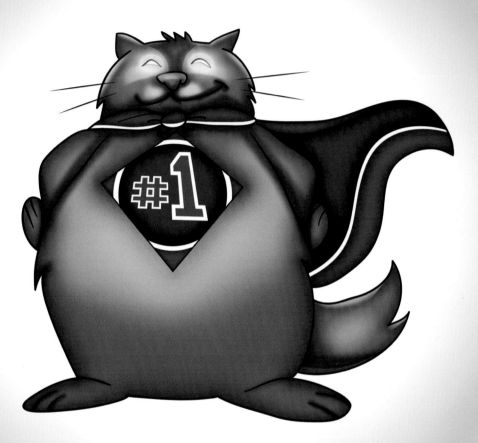

MEANING: Something that is **top notch** is the best.

ORIGIN: The origin of this phrase is uncertain. It likely comes from a game or activity that involved notches.

EXAMPLE: Jamal's pinball playing was **top notch**. He could score a million points without even trying.

EGG ON YOUR FACE

MEANING: If you have **egg on your face**, you are embarrassed after a mistake.

ORIGIN: This phrase may come from having egg on your face after eating. It might refer to farm dogs that are caught eating chickens' eggs. Or, it might come from theatergoers throwing eggs at actors during a bad play.

EXAMPLE: Naomi had **egg on her face** after writing her book report about the wrong book.

IN YOUR WHEELHOUSE

MEANING: Something that is within your area of knowledge is **in your wheelhouse**.

ORIGIN: In baseball, the area of the strike zone where the batter can hit the ball best is known as the wheelhouse. The term may come from the powerful motion of a train wheelhouse, which rotates a locomotive on a large platform.

EXAMPLE: The planets unit in science class was right **in Vanessa's wheelhouse**. She loved reading about space.

GREEN THUMB

MEANING: A person with a **green thumb** is very good at gardening.

ORIGIN: This phrase may have come from gardeners holding clay pots with green algae on them. This would turn their thumbs green after working for a long time.

EXAMPLE: Antonio had a **green thumb**. He grew the best vegetables on his block.

PULL THE WOOL OVER YOUR EYES

MEANING: If someone deceives you, he or she **pulls the wool over your eyes**.

ORIGIN: The origin of this idiom is not known for certain. It may come from the tradition of judges in the 1700s wearing wigs made of wool. If you pulled the wigs over their eyes, they would be unable to see the facts of a case.

EXAMPLE: Mariah's parents **pulled the wool over her eyes**. They told her they were taking her to the dentist, but they actually went to a carnival.

WORTH A HILL OF BEANS

MEANING: Something that is **worth a hill of beans** has very little value.

ORIGIN: This phrase was originally used to refer to actual bean plants. Later, it took on the meaning of *beans* as worthless.

EXAMPLE: Beatrice's big coat was **worth a hill of beans** in this hot weather.

TOE THE LINE

MEANING: When someone goes along with standards or rules, they **toe the line**.

ORIGIN: This phrase refers to people lining up along a marked line on the ground. It comes from similar phrases from the 1800s, such as *toe the mark* and *toe the scratch*.

EXAMPLE: Darren felt it was very important to **toe the line** in the science lab.

WHEN PIGS FLY

MEANING: If something is unlikely or ridiculous, people say it will happen **when pigs fly**.

ORIGIN: This phrase compares the ridiculous idea of pigs flying to another ridiculous idea. It comes from a Scottish proverb.

EXAMPLE: Kylie was always on time for school. Her friends said she would be late **when pigs fly**.

ON THE BALL

MEANING: Someone who is alert and aware is **on the ball**.

ORIGIN: This idiom is a shortened version of a phrase used in many sports: "keep your eye on the ball."

EXAMPLE: Wyatt was **on the ball** with food safety. He always checked the expiration date on the package before he ate anything.

DON'T HAVE A COW

MEANING: If you tell someone "**Don't have a cow**," you are telling them not to get too excited.

ORIGIN: This phrase compares someone acting dramatic with someone giving birth to a cow. It was made popular by a character on the television show *The Simpsons*. An older variation of the phrase was, "Don't have a cat."

EXAMPLE: Taylor's friend was upset that their Frisbee had landed on a roof. "**Don't have a cow**," Taylor said. "I have another one in my garage."

CUT AND RUN

MEANING: If you **cut and run**, you leave somewhere quickly, usually while retreating.

ORIGIN: This phrase probably comes from sailing ships. When sailors had to escape quickly in emergencies, there was no time to pull the anchor back up. Instead, they would cut the cable and leave as quickly as they could.

EXAMPLE: Todd's kickball team was losing by ten points, but there was no way they would **cut and run**.

PUT ON THE BACK BURNER

MEANING: Something that is **put on the back burner** is put off for a while so that more important things can be done.

ORIGIN: This phrase refers to cooking on a stove top with burners in the front and back. If something you are cooking needs extra attention, you put it on a front burner so it is easier to get to. Things that you can leave for a while can be put on the back burner.

EXAMPLE: Amy loved her ukulele, but she had to **put it on the back burner**. Right now, she had to study for her geology test.

HOISTED BY YOUR OWN PETARD

MEANING: If you are **hoisted by your own petard**, you are defeated by your own plans.

ORIGIN: A petard was a medieval weapon. It was a small bomb used to break open gates and walls. If something went wrong, the person lighting the bomb would be blown, or hoisted, into the air.

EXAMPLE: Vivian was **hoisted by her own petard**. She tried to knock down her brother's sandcastle, but she tripped and fell over the one she built herself.

THROW YOUR HAT
IN THE RING

MEANING: If you **throw your hat in the ring**, you enter a competition or contest.

ORIGIN: This phrase comes from boxing. Boxers would throw their hats into the boxing ring to challenge someone.

EXAMPLE: Troy decided to **throw his hat in the ring**. He would play piano in the talent show.

BATS IN THE BELFRY

MEANING: If someone has **bats in the belfry**, they are crazy or eccentric.

ORIGIN: A belfry is a bell tower. Here, it refers to a person's head. The idea is that if you have bats flying around in your belfry, you are crazy.

EXAMPLE: The mad scientist in the movie had **bats in the belfry**.

GO AGAINST THE GRAIN

MEANING: If you **go against the grain**, you do something unusual or something you wouldn't typically do.

ORIGIN: This phrase refers to the grain of a piece of wood. It is easier to go with the grain than against it when working with wood.

EXAMPLE: Elias **went against the grain** when choosing his clothing. He always wore long, colorful scarves, even in the summer.

BIG KAHUNA

MEANING: The **big kahuna** is the most important person or thing in a group.

ORIGIN: This phrase comes from the Hawaiian word *kahuna* meaning a wizard. It was first used in the 1959 movie *Gidget*.

EXAMPLE: Allison was the **big kahuna** in her school chess club.

SNAKE OIL

MEANING: Someone who sells a product they say is miraculous but is actually worthless is selling **snake oil**.

ORIGIN: Traveling medicine salespeople would try to trick people into buying medicines they claimed would cure any disease. One of these medicines was snake oil.

EXAMPLE: Jasmine could tell whenever a television commercial was selling **snake oil**.

WAIT FOR THE OTHER SHOE TO DROP

MEANING: When you **wait for the other shoe to drop**, you are waiting for a consequence to happen.

ORIGIN: This phrase comes from a joke. A man comes home to his apartment late at night. He takes off his shoes and drops the first one to the floor loudly. He is more careful with the second shoe, setting it down softly. After a few minutes, his neighbor bangs on the wall, yelling, "Drop the other shoe already!"

EXAMPLE: Stephanie was **waiting for the other shoe to drop**. A character in the novel she was reading robbed a bank. She was sure he would be caught soon.

SQUARE MEAL

MEANING: A **square meal** is a complete meal.

ORIGIN: In the 1500s, *square* meant fair or complete. The phrase comes from the United States more recently. It is related to the phrases *fair and square* and *square deal*.

EXAMPLE: Jade was sure to always eat three **square meals** each day.

HAM IT UP

MEANING: If you **ham it up**, you act in an overly dramatic way.

ORIGIN: This phrase comes from an earlier word, *hamfatter*, which meant a bad actor. Some have said this evolved from the word ham fat, or lard, which was used to remove stage makeup. However, there is little evidence for that.

EXAMPLE: Dana thought it was funny when actors in movies really **hammed it up**.

PUT UP YOUR DUKES

MEANING: When you **put up your dukes**, you raise your fists and get ready to fight.

ORIGIN: *Duke* is slang for hand or fist. The source of this is uncertain. It may come from British slang.

EXAMPLE: The bad guy in the movie was always telling people to **put up their dukes**.

PECKING ORDER

MEANING: A **pecking order** is the ranking of the importance of people in a group.

ORIGIN: In groups of chickens, higher-ranking chickens peck lower-ranking ones.

EXAMPLE: Malik was glad that there wasn't a clear **pecking order** on the playground. Everybody treated everyone else fairly.

MONDAY-MORNING QUARTERBACK

MEANING: A person who is a **Monday-morning quarterback** gives their advice on something they don't know about after it is too late to change it.

ORIGIN: In American football, most games are played on Sundays. The quarterback is the leader of each team. A fan who talks on Monday about what should've been done on Sunday is too late to do anything about it.

EXAMPLE: Hector was being a **Monday-morning quarterback**. After his friend Raven lost the tennis match, he told her where she should've hit the ball.

IT'S NOT ROCKET SCIENCE

MEANING: When a subject being talked about is easy to understand, people say **it's not rocket science**.

ORIGIN: This phrase comes from the fact that rocket science is very difficult.

EXAMPLE: Diego liked to show his friends how to build model trains. "Don't worry. **It's not rocket science**," he said.

BULLY PULPIT

MEANING: When someone uses the power of his or her position to spread their message, they are using a **bully pulpit**.

ORIGIN: This phrase uses an older meaning of *bully*, best or excellent. A pulpit is the place where a public speaker stands, usually in a church. US President Theodore Roosevelt coined this idiom.

EXAMPLE: Selena used her **bully pulpit** on the student council to talk about the rising cost of milk.

THE DIE IS CAST

MEANING: If it's too late to change the outcome of something, the **die has been cast**.

ORIGIN: You can't change the outcome after tossing dice. The phrase was used by the Roman general Julius Caesar as he decided to overthrow the Roman government.

EXAMPLE: The die was cast when Mallory said the last letter of her word in the spelling bee.

PYRRHIC VICTORY

MEANING: A victory won at a very high cost is a **Pyrrhic victory**.

ORIGIN: This idiom comes from the Greek King Pyrrhus, who battled the Romans in 279 BC. His army won the battle, but they lost a huge number of soldiers.

EXAMPLE: Jonah's baseball team won the game, but it was a **Pyrrhic victory**. Their star pitcher hurt his arm, and their best batter sprained her ankle.

About the Author

Arnold Ringstad lives in Minneapolis, where he graduated from the University of Minnesota in 2011. He enjoys reading books about space exploration and playing board games with his girlfriend. Writing about idioms makes him as happy as a clam.

About the Illustrator

Dan McGeehan loves being an illustrator. His art appears in many magazines and children's books. He currently lives in Oklahoma.